THE THAMES from a

CONTENTS

INTRODUCTION

The River Thames carves a path across southern England from west to east for 346km (215 miles). It rises in the Cotswolds in Gloucestershire: from there the river goes on to form the boundaries between Gloucestershire and Wiltshire, Oxfordshire and Berkshire, Buckinghamshire and Berkshire, Surrey and Greater London, Essex and Kent. The two claimed sources are springs that both rise high in the Cotswolds of Gloucestershire. The Thames is not the longest river in Great Britain – that title belongs to the River Severn which is 354km (220 miles) long. The Thames, however, is the longest river wholly in England. The river cuts through London where the tides change the direction of the river twice a day as far up as Teddington, a distance of 110km (68 miles). In the days before the river traffic was motorised this change of flow was useful to cargo boats. But it also brought seasonal floods when heavy rainfall upstream caused high river spates that combined with the powerful spring tides.

Back in 1624, the river was navigable by barges as far upstream as Oxford. Locks constructed above Staines in 1771, and between Staines and Teddington between 1810-15 made passage even easier. Flow control was achieved through a combination of weirs and locks, and in 1982 the Thames Barrier, downstream from the City of London, became operational. Today between Lechlade and Teddington there are forty-eight pound locks and more than forty-eight weirs. The weirs ensure a reasonable flow of water throughout the year by conserving water in the upper reaches to supplement the drier months. London's inhabitants and industry make huge demands on the river for water supply. Down the centuries the Thames also carried sewage to the sea, causing severe pollution until as recently as fifty years ago. Now, improved methods of sewage treatment and control of industrial effluent have cleaned up the river to a great extent and the wildlife is gradually filtering back as the environment improves.

When Julius Caesar invaded Britain in 55BC he wrote in *De Bello Gallico* of the river *Tamesis*. Isis, the name still given to the river upstream of Oxford, may just be an abbreviation of the Latin name.

The Thames Path was officially launched as a national trail on July 24, 1996. The path follows the River Thames, mostly along the old Thames towpath, from its source all the way to the Thames Barrier in London. Unlike other long distance paths in Britain, the Thames route is the first to follow a river for its entire length and pass through the heart of dense urban areas.

Photographs from top to bottom: near Lechlade, Temple Island, Millennium Wheel, Thames Haven

Photographs, text and design by Adrian Warren and Dae Sasitorn

MYRIAD BOOKS LIMITED

THAMES HEAD
Gloucestershire (above left)

N 51... 41.664'   W 002... 01.768'

The official source of the River Thames lies at Thames Head in the Cotswolds, in Gloucestershire. Thames Head is 4.8km (3 miles) south-west of Cirencester, in a field called Trewsbury Mead, 118m above sea level. There an ancient ash tree grows by a stony hollow in the ground from which the river springs to flow down the sloping meadow. It is marked by a block of stone with the inscription:

*The Conservators of the River Thames
1857 - 1974
This stone was placed here to mark the
Source of the River Thames*

As can be seen from our photograph, it often dries up and **the first water visible from the air (left)** was several hundred metres further down, close to the Fosse Way, the old Roman road to Tetbury, not far from Kemble.

****

SEVEN SPRINGS
Gloucestershire (above right)

N 51... 51.063'   W 002... 03.029'

As with many rivers, the actual source is controversial. The unofficial source of the Thames is 17.5km (11 miles) away from Thames Head at Seven Springs, in the parish of Coberley, Gloucestershire. Here, some 8km (5 miles) south of Cheltenham, the river Churn rises to flow south-eastwards to join the other headwaters near Cricklade. Seven Springs, at 200m above sea level, is much higher than Thames Head, and is much further from the estuary, adding some 14.5km (9 miles) to the official length of the river. Here, in a hollow by a busy road, a small stream appears briefly from its underground passage and there is a stone with an inscription in Latin: *Hic tuus o pater Tamesine septemgeminus fons.*

****

KEMBLE, Gloucestershire (above)

Kemble lies to the south of the town of Cirencester and next to the village lies an important ex-military airfield. At the end of 1939 there were already well over 600 aircraft here, most of which were Hurricanes. The Red Arrows came along with the Central Flying School during the 1960s. An amazing array of historic aircraft can now be seen at Kemble as well as the newly opened Bristol Aero Collection Museum and popular fly-ins that are held at regular intervals throughout the year.

****

KEMPSFORD, Gloucestershire (left)

Kempsford is a small village by the River Thames and lies next to RAF Fairford, seen in the photograph. The airfield was constructed in 1944 for British and American troop carriers and gliders that were used during the D-Day invasion of Normandy. After the war, the base was transferred to the US Air Force for strategic bomber operations. The airfield's 3,000m runway is today the longest in the UK, and designated as a trans-Atlantic abort landing site for the space shuttle. Officially an RAF station, this is one of the airfields currently used by the United States Air Forces in Europe. B1b Lancer bombers were deployed from here during the Kosovo crisis, and B52s against Iraq.

****

LECHLADE, Gloucestershire

Upstream from Lechlade (above), the Thames is still a small river. At **Lechlade (left)** however, the tributaries Leach and Coln flow into the Thames. Stone for the dome of St. Paul's cathedral was loaded on to barges here in the late 17th century. The village remains largely unspoilt with a large number of Georgian houses. The spire of the 15th century church dedicated to St. Lawrence dominates the village. **The Thames downstream from Lechlade (near Buscot, above right)** is remarkable for its lack of houses but this is due to the tendency to flooding in the winter. For a distance of 45km (28 miles), there is peaceful, open countryside with kingfishers and waterfowl, punctuated by a few lock cottages and inns.

****

RADCOT, Oxfordshire (left)

At Radcot the Thames divides into three channels around two small islands. Here a bridge carries the road from Witney to Faringdon across the river. It was built around 1154 and is the oldest on the river. Over the centuries there have been many bloody clashes to control this ancient crossing point. In 1141 King Stephen defeated the forces of Matilda, Queen of Anjou, who had built a castle to the north of the bridge. The barons fought King John here in 1387 and the Civil War saw several more skirmishes. On one of the islands there is a pub which dates from 1873.

****

THE THAMES AT SWINFORD
Oxfordshire (left)

The bridge at Swinford has been a toll crossing for close on 1,000 years. Originally it was a *swine ford*, a ford where pigs could cross the river. The bridge was built in 1769 after George III got wet while crossing. It is now one of two remaining toll bridges over the Thames. Here the river meanders through lush green meadows. Nearby Farmoor Reservoir is the largest single area of open water in the county. It is the home of Oxford Sailing Club and is a popular bird watching site. The two large concrete basins attract overflying migrant birds, and many rarities have been seen there.

****

OXFORD, Oxfordshire (right)

The great university town of Oxford is rich in history and architecture. Here was a ford across the Thames used by cattle farmers to drive their oxen to market. The university is the second oldest in Europe after the Sorbonne in Paris. The traditional towers and spires so characteristic of Oxford now share the skyline with the rectangular blocks of modern buildings. On the southern edge of the city the Thames is joined by the river Cherwell which flows under the famous Magdalen bridge. At Iffley there is the first pound lock built on the Thames during the reign of James I.

****

ABINGDON
Oxfordshire (left)

Abingdon is an old market town. It lies next to lush green water meadows where the river Ock, bringing water from the Vale of the White Horse, joins the Thames. It is reputed to be the oldest continually occupied settlement in England. The town originally grew and prospered as a result of its abbey, founded in 676. During the reign of Henry VIII the town's economy was devastated when much of the abbey was demolished. Today however the town's Monday Market, established well before 1328, continues to thrive.

****

CLIFTON HAMPDEN, Oxfordshire (above)

At Clifton Hampden the Thames is crossed by a six-ribbed arched brick bridge designed by George Gilbert Scott in 1864. Here the river forms the border between Oxfordshire and Berkshire. This small village has several attractive Elizabethan cottages. After a visit to Oxford in 1862 the Lord Mayor of London's state barge ran aground here, and in the winter of 1891 the river was so frozen that a sheep roast was held on the ice.

****

WALLINGFORD, Oxfordshire (left)

In early times, Wallingford was the site of a ford across the Thames. Today it is spanned by an elegant many-arched bridge. The Romans and the Anglo-Saxons settled here. They fortified the town and the ramparts are still visible. The town became an important hub for trading routes and the setting for many battles. In 871, Danish invaders were defeated close by; then in 1006, the Danes destroyed Wallingford. Some castle ruins can still be seen. In the 12th century, the Treaty of Wallingford gave Henry II the throne, and in 1155 the king gave the town its first charter. During the Civil War, the town was the last Royalist stronghold to surrender, but the Parliamentary forces destroyed it so thoroughly that only fragments of it remained.

****

GORING

Oxfordshire (right)

The village of Goring is sited at an important crossing point, where the Romans built a causeway to ford the river. It is an Area of Outstanding Natural Beauty and with its riverside location Goring is a popular tourist centre. Large numbers of boats moor along the towpath during the summer months. The river was always a major highway and power source for water mills. In the 17th century, interest in Thames navigation grew as the expansion of London demanded ever more commodities, much of which reached the capital by river. However, locks and a good flow of water were necessary. In 1787, pound locks replaced the flash locks at Goring and Cleeve. Downstream from Goring, the River Thames has broken through the hills and now makes its way south-eastwards towards London.

****

GORING GAP

Oxfordshire (below)

With Goring in the distance, the Thames emerges from the Goring Gap in a wide majestic sweep just upstream from Pangbourne. The Gap is an interesting geological feature, dividing the Berkshire Downs from the Chiltern Hills.

****

PANGBOURNE
Berkshire

At Pangbourne (left) there is a bridge and also a weir. The river now runs eastwards along the base of the Chilterns for some 3 km through **pleasant meadows (below)** to head towards Reading. Kenneth Grahame, author of *Wind in the Willows*, lived in Pangbourne, and this stretch of the river was said to be the inspiration for E H Shepherd's illustrations.

****

MAPLEDURHAM
Berkshire (right)

Michael Blunt built the impressive Tudor manor, Mapledurham Court, where he entertained Queen Elizabeth I. The water mill adjoining the manor is also 16th century. The poet Alexander Pope often visited the manor in the early 18th century. The grounds by the Thames are the background to John Galsworthy's *The Forsyte Saga* and Kenneth Grahame's *Wind in the Willows*.

****

READING, Berkshire (left)

Strategically placed on the Thames, Reading has always been important. The town was a centre of the textile industry in the Middle Ages. It was also a place of pilgrimage – Henry I founded the abbey in 1121 and was later buried here. During the Dissolution under Henry VIII the last abbot was hanged at the gates. The 19th century saw the rise of biscuits and beer as staple industries of the town. Reading prison's most famous inmate was Oscar Wilde, who subsequently wrote *The Ballad of Reading Gaol* in 1898.

****

SHIPLAKE WEIR, Oxfordshire and WARGRAVE, Berkshire (above)

The villages of Shiplake and Wargrave lie on opposite banks of the Thames upstream of Henley. A Regatta is held here in early August. This charming stretch of the river is very popular during summer weekends with boating enthusiasts. Jerome K Jerome mentioned Shiplake in his book *Three Men in a Boat* (1889).

****

HENLEY-ON-THAMES, Oxfordshire (left)

Henley-on-Thames lies at the foot of the Chiltern Hills. The old town was incorporated in 1526, has a medieval church and a wide market street flanked by Georgian buildings. Henley is probably most famous for the annual Royal Regatta, which was established in 1839. This is a five-day event of rowing races and social gatherings. The races are held on the longest naturally straight stretch of river in Britain and the regulation course distance is 2,100m (1 mile 550 yards).

****

TEMPLE ISLAND, Oxfordshire (above)

Temple Island is situated 2.4km (1.5 miles) downstream from Henley, on one of the most beautiful stretches of the River Thames. Surrounded by water meadows and wooded hills, it marks the starting point of the famous Henley Royal Regatta course. The temple itself is a delightful folly, designed by James Wyatt as a fishing lodge for the Christopher Wren mansion, Fawley Court, on Henley Reach. The temple was built in 1771, and its Etruscan style interior was based on designs found at Pompeii.

****

MARLOW, Buckinghamshire (left)

At Marlow the Thames forms the dividing line between Buckinghamshire and Berkshire. There has been a bridge across the Thames at Marlow since 1227. The present bridge with its main span of 72m was built in 1831 to replace a wooden bridge sited further downstream. In 1965, the bridge was restored but as a safety measure the weight restriction now in effect bans lorries from crossing the bridge.

****

BARN ELMS WATER WORKS & HAMMERSMITH BRIDGE, (right)

An oasis of green, Barn Elms Water Works lies on the south bank of the Thames just downstream from Hammersmith Bridge, which can be seen in the distance. The ornamental bridge, much loved by Londoners, was designed by Sir Joseph Bazalgette and built in 1887. It is now protected as a monument.

****

PUTNEY BRIDGE
(below)

Putney Bridge was also designed by Sir Joseph Bazalgette and was built in 1886 from solid Cornish granite. Just downriver is a combined rail and footbridge.

****

BATTERSEA HELIPORT (above right)

Battersea heliport is currently owned by Harrods Holdings, best known as owners of the famous department store.

BATTERSEA BRIDGE
(below right)

During the 18th century Battersea and Chelsea were connected only by ferry. A wooden bridge was built in 1771 allowing pedestrians and wagons to cross the Thames. However, the design featured many wooden piers and spans. This was notoriously dangerous at night or during foggy weather, and boats regularly collided with it. It was eventually replaced in 1886 with the cast iron arches of Battersea Bridge.

****

MILLENNIUM WHEEL (next page)

The Millennium Wheel, also known as the London Eye, at 135m high is the world's tallest observation wheel and the fourth tallest structure in London. It was built to celebrate the turn of the millennium and cost some £20 million. The wheel is an impressive feat of engineering but its installation at Jubilee Gardens opposite Westminster proved to be far more complex than the engineers had anticipated. To raise the wheel from a horizontal position, where it extended out across part of the Thames, to its final vertical position was painstakingly slow and hampered by cable failures. Now it can carry 800 passengers at any one time in its 32 transparent pods, which offer spectacular views of London. A single revolution of the wheel takes approximately 30 minutes.

****

BATTERSEA POWER STATION (right)

The British architect Giles Gilbert Scott designed Battersea Power Station with a sumptuous Art Deco control room, Italian marble turbine hall, polished parquet floors, wrought iron staircases and four characteristic white smokestacks. The largest brick building in Europe, the power station provided London with electricity from 1937 to 1980. Now the forlorn hulk of Battersea Power Station awaits its future fate. The idea of a power station in London was controversial from the outset and fears of pollution resulted in a storm of protest in 1927. Today Battersea Power Station is one of London's best loved landmarks, and there is just as much controversy over its future.

****

BATTERSEA PARK and PEACE PAGODA (left)

Battersea Park was created in the 1850s from marshy wasteland. Earth excavated during the building of Victoria Dock was carried here on barges to raise the ground level. This pleasant park is now famous for its flowers, waterfalls and landscaping. Its Peace Pagoda was the first to be built in any western capital. Japanese Buddhist nuns and monks built it in 1985 to provide a focus for people of all races and creeds, uniting them in the search for peace.

****

VAUXHALL BRIDGE and MI6 BUILDING (right)

The MI6 building on the south bank of the Thames and an apartment block on the Wandsworth Road overlook Vauxhall Bridge. Sir Alexander Binnie's late 19th century design replaced James Walker's original cast-iron bridge. It was completed in 1906, with five steel supporting arches on masonry piers. From the river you have the best view of the bridge's ornamental bronze reliefs representing industry and agriculture on one side, with government, the arts and education on the other.

****

LAMBETH PALACE and LAMBETH BRIDGE (left)

For nearly 800 years Lambeth Palace has been the residence of Archbishops of Canterbury. The magnificent red-brick Tudor gateway was built in 1490 by Cardinal Morton. Lambeth Palace, Hampton Court and the Tower of London are the only palaces sited on the banks of the Thames. Archbishops moored their state barges here in readiness for river trips to Westminster or Whitehall. Along the wall of the Great Hall is a fig tree originally planted by Cardinal Pole in the 16th century. The palace has been visited by kings and queens, attacked by Wat Tyler's rebels, invaded by Cromwell's army and bombed by German aircraft. It has also been used as a prison for non-believers in the Catholic faith and is the place where Cranmer composed the Book of Common Prayer.

Lambeth Bridge boasts one of the best upstream views of any London bridge. Its steel arches link Lambeth Palace to Millbank and Westminster. The bridge features five spans.

****

WESTMINSTER (above)

The Houses of Parliament, otherwise known as the Palace of Westminster, stand on the site of a royal palace built by King Canute. Later rebuilt by Edward the Confessor, the palace remained the royal residence until Henry VIII moved to Whitehall. Although the buildings have been burned and rebuilt several times they have been the meeting place for parliament for centuries. These neo-Gothic style buildings on the banks of the Thames were designed by Charles Barry and the artist Augustus Pugin in 1840, and have become a symbol for Britain today. Bombed by the Germans during World War II, the buildings were carefully restored. **The tower of Big Ben** is nearly 100m tall and the clock dials 7m across. The great bell weighs 13.5 tons and was cast in Whitechapel in 1858. **Westminster Bridge** originally opened in 1750 and established one of the most important links across the Thames. Widely praised at the time, the bridge stood for over 70 years before structural checks revealed problems with the its foundations. Although remedial works were carried out, the government subsequently decided to construct a new bridge. The task of designing it was awarded to Thomas Page and Charles Barry, and the current bridge was opened in 1862. Today it is one of London's busiest bridges, connecting Westminster to Waterloo and the new attraction of the London Eye.

****

CHARING CROSS (right)

Charing Cross is one of the great Victorian railway stations and was opened in 1864. The station was built to extend the Southern Eastern Railway westward from London Bridge and to transport passengers from Kent into the centre of London. On the forecourt of the station stands the Eleanor Cross, one of nine put up by King Edward I in memory of Queen Eleanor. The original was made of wood and the present one was designed in 1863 to replicate as closely as possible the medieval one. The cross is the point from which Britain measures its road distances to and from London.

****

ROYAL FESTIVAL HALL
(left)

The Royal Festival Hall is situated on the south bank of the Thames between Hungerford and Waterloo Bridges. Part of the South Bank cultural complex, the Hall was designed by Robert Matthew and Leslie Martin and was originally built for the Festival of Britain in 1951. The auditorium seats 3,000 and its acoustics have been praised by many. The Festival Hall was one of the first concert halls in the world to be built using the application of scientific principles to acoustic behaviour in its original design.

****

A CHAIN OF BRIDGES (left)

Looking east from Blackfriars Bridge to Millennium Bridge, Southwark Bridge, Cannon Street Railway, London Bridge, and in the distance Tower Bridge. For centuries London Bridge was the only crossing over the river in this area. The Romans built a wooden bridge later replaced in stone. During the Elizabethan era London Bridge was topped with timber houses along its length, with a gatehouse at the Southwark end that displayed the severed heads of traitors following executions. The houses were removed from the bridge in the 18th century and a new bridge opened in 1831. That was sold to an American businessman in the 1960s who reassembled it piece by piece in the desert of Texas. Work on its replacement was completed in 1972.

****

MILLENNIUM BRIDGE (right)

London's Millennium Bridge was the first pedestrian crossing to be built over the Thames in central London for more than a century. It is a 325m long steel structure between Southwark and Blackfriars bridges, linking the City of London at St. Paul's Cathedral with the Tate Modern Gallery at Bankside. The bridge, which opened on June 10, 2000, is a very shallow suspension bridge: its three spans are propped by two river supports. Pedestrians have unrivalled views of London high above the Thames. The architect Lord Foster described the bridge as a "blade of light" when lit at night. It is a spectacular addition to London's cityscape.

****

THE CITY (right)

The City is where London began. The Romans called it Londinium, built a stone wall around it, turned it into a port and built London Bridge. Through the Middle Ages, London flourished and by the 17th century the city was expanding rapidly. Then came the horrors of the plague, followed a year later by the Great Fire which burned some 13,200 houses, 84 churches and St Paul's in just four days. Rebuilt, London kept on expanding, with the City itself always the commercial centre. Further terrible devastation came during the air raids of World War II, and in the second half of the 20th century recovery was accompanied by the building of clusters of high-rise blocks. The railway station is Cannon Street, and the bridge on the right is the modern London Bridge.

****

TOWER OF LONDON (left)

A prison and place of execution, the Tower of London was also a royal palace, an armoury, a treasury, an observatory, a mint and even a zoo. Cromwell demolished the palace, the observatory went to Greenwich in 1675, the Royal Mint moved out in 1810, and the Victorians moved the zoo. The Tower is a national treasure with a chilling history of suffering and deaths that have taken place within its walls. Originally the site of a Saxon fort William the Conqueror built the White Tower to protect London and to instil fear in his subjects. Over the centuries more walls and towers were added to provide a maze of passageways, dark cells and secret tunnels. The last prisoner to be held at the Tower was Hitler's deputy, Rudolf Hess, in 1941.

****

TOWER BRIDGE (above and front cover)

This famous symbol of London was, until recently, the last bridge downstream across the Thames. For centuries London Bridge was the only crossing over the Thames in London. As the city grew, more bridges were built upstream, but not downstream since that area was busy with shipping. By the 19th century, London's East End was so densely populated that a bridge was urgently needed. Tower Bridge was designed with two hydraulically operated bascules that lift to allow ships to pass. The two 43m supporting towers have high-level walkways for pedestrians to cross when the bascules were raised. It was completed in 1894, after 8 years of construction. Then all that was needed was to signal the duty watchmen as the ship approached. Now, the bascules still lift several times a week but advance notice is required.

****

MILLENNIUM DOME (above)

To mark the birth of a new millennium the controversial dome was built as the focal point of London's New Year 2000 celebrations. Just a short distance from the Greenwich Royal Observatory it is on the line where Greenwich Mean Time ushers in the new year. This is the largest single structure in the UK and cost over £50 million. At 320m in diameter and 50m high, it is tall enough to accommodate Nelson's column, large enough to contain 13 Albert Halls, 2 Wembley stadiums, or the Great Pyramid at Giza. It was open for just one year as a showcase of the achievements of the last 1,000 years and is now closed to visitors.

****

GREENWICH & CUTTY SARK (left)

After the death of the Duke of Gloucester in 1447, the manor of Greenwich passed to the Crown and became a royal palace for 200 years. Henry VIII was born here as were his daughters Mary and Elizabeth. In 1694 a charter established the Greenwich hospital for the relief and support of seamen and their dependants and for the improvement of navigation, and it later became the Royal Naval College. The Royal Observatory, on the Greenwich Meridian sets world time (Greenwich Mean Time) and place (Greenwich Meridian). In 1884 an international convention agreed that all countries would adopt a universal Mean Solar Day, beginning at the Mean Midnight at Greenwich and counted on a 24 hour clock. The Meridian Line, known as zero longitude, is a theoretical line running from the North Pole to the South Pole, through the Observatory at Greenwich. All other lines of longitude are measured from here. Nearby is the elegant Cutty Sark, the last surviving tea-clipper, which was built at Dumbarton in 1869 just as steam and the opening of the Suez Canal were making sailing ships redundant.

****

DOCKS & CITY AIRPORT (right)

Royal Victoria Dock, Royal Albert Dock and King George V Docks surround London City, the nearest airport to central London. Docklands is an area with a rich and diverse history. In recent years it has been transformed into a vibrant business and social centre with over 1.25 million visitors a year. Docklands boasts a number of attractions for visitors including Canary Wharf and the London Arena.

****

THAMES BARRIER
(left)

The Thames Barrier is an ingenious piece of engineering. Its purpose is to protect London from flooding due to surge tides or a general rise in sea level due to changes in weather and the melting of polar ice caps. The design of the barrier allows for ships to pass freely in and out of the docks in London, but in times of dangerously high water, the barrier can be closed with huge steel gates each weighing up to 1,500 tonnes. The piers are founded on solid chalk, over 15m below the level of the river. Work on the barrier started in 1974 and was opened by Elizabeth II on May 8, 1984. The scheme cost nearly £500 million.

****

LONDON, as seen from DARTFORD (below)

The view looking up the Thames towards Erith Marshes, Thamesmead and, in the distance, the City of London.

****

DARTFORD CROSSING (left)

The Queen Elizabeth II Bridge at Dartford opened in 1991. It is 450m long and is Europe's largest cable supported bridge. It is the only bridge downstream of Tower Bridge. The tallest liners can pass under the central span. It took 3 years to build and cost £86 million, money raised by private companies which will be paid back by tolls. There are two other crossings of the River Thames at this point, both of which are tunnels.

****

SHEERNESS, ISLE OF SHEPPEY (right)

Sheppey was known for sheep rearing in the past. Sheerness is a commercial port at the mouth of the River Medway and main town of the Isle of Sheppey. Samuel Pepys established a Royal Navy dockyard here in the 17th century and it served the navy until 1960. Since then Sheerness has become one of the fastest expanding ports in the UK. It is the largest point of import for motor vehicles.

****

THAMES HAVEN (above)

A ship passes the oil refinery at Thames Haven, heading towards the Thames estuary.

****

SOUTHEND-ON-SEA

Southend (right) was once the most popular holiday resort for Londoners. In the early 19th century the villages of Eastwood, Leigh, Prittlewell, Shoebury and Southchurch started to expand along the shores of the Thames estuary and Southend evolved. Today it is home for thousands of commuters who work in London every day.

Southend pier (above) is almost 2.5km (1.5 miles) long, the longest in the world. In World War II, 3,367 convoys (84,297 ships) sailed from here.

****

MINSTER, ISLE OF SHEPPEY and THE THAMES ESTUARY (above)

Minster overlooks the safe landing areas around Sheerness and Queenborough. There was a settlement here in Roman times, and in the Middle Ages the island was a significant lookout point. The abbey on Sheppey was founded in AD644. Legend has it that when the Vikings landed on Sheerness beach on one of their first raids on England, they were so impressed by the serenity of the nuns that they left them in peace.

****

LAST REFUGE Ltd

Nature is a precious inheritance, to be cared for and cherished by all of us. Last Refuge Ltd is a small company primarily dedicated to documenting and archiving endangered environments and species in our rapidly changing world, through films, images and research. The company was established in 1992, while studying wild giant pandas in the Qinling mountains of central China, which seemed, literally, to be the "last refuge" for these charismatic animals. The company's name was adopted for that project and it seemed logical to continue with it, embracing new projects worldwide. Two films on lemurs in Madagascar quickly followed and the ring-tailed lemur became the company's logo. Adrian Warren and Dae Sasitorn, who run the company out of a farmhouse in Somerset, have created a special web site, www.lastrefuge.co.uk, in order to present their work, which is becoming a huge resource for information, and an extensive photographic archive of still and moving images for both education and media. Ultimately they hope to offer special conservation awards to fund work by others.

ADRIAN WARREN

Adrian Warren is a biologist, and a commercial pilot, with over thirty years experience as a photographer and filmmaker, working worldwide for the BBC Natural History Unit, and as a director in the IMAX giant screen format. He has recently designed a new wing mount camera system for aircraft to further develop his interest in aviation, aerial filming and photography. As a stills photographer, he has a personal photographic archive of over 100,000 pictures, with worldwide coverage of wildlife, landscapes, aerials, and peoples. His photographs appear in books, magazines, advertisements, posters, calendars, greetings cards and many other products. His awards include a Winston Churchill Fellowship; the Cherry Kearton Medal from the Royal Geographical Society in London; the Genesis award from the Ark Trust for Conservation; an International Prime Time Emmy; and the Golden Eagle Award from New York.

DAE SASITORN

Dae Sasitorn is an academic from the world of chemistry but has given it up to follow her love for nature. She manages the company and has created and designed the Last Refuge website as well as scanning thousands of images for the archive. She has also become a first-class photographer in her own right.

THE PHOTOGRAPHY

Adrian and Dae operate their own Cessna 182G out of a tiny farm strip close to their house. They bought the single engined four-seater aircraft in May 1999 in order to develop a new wing mounted camera system for cinematography. The 1964 Cessna was in beautiful condition, and had only one previous owner. It is the perfect aircraft for aerial work: small, manoeuvrable, with plenty of power, and the high wing configuration offering an almost unrestricted view on the world below. With twenty degrees of flap it is possible to fly as slowly as sixty knots. The cabin side window opens upwards and outwards and is kept open by the air flow. Over London, however, where it is not permitted to fly a single engine fixed wing aircraft in case of engine failure, the Cessna had to be abandoned in favour of a helicopter equipped with floats.

The photographs were taken on Hasselblad medium format 6x6cm cameras and lenses (mostly 50mm) using Fujichrome Velvia film. Waiting for the right weather, with a clear atmosphere and less than fifty per cent cloud cover, required being on standby for months.

First Published in 2003 by Myriad Books Limited,
35 Bishopsthorpe Road, London, SE26

ISBN 1 904154 39 5

Designed by Dae Sasitorn and Adrian Warren
Last Refuge Limited
Printed in China

LAST REFUGE Ltd

Nature is a precious inheritance, to be cared for and cherished by all of us. Last Refuge Ltd is a small company primarily dedicated to documenting and archiving endangered environments and species in our rapidly changing world, through films, images and research. The company was established in 1992 for a study of wild giant pandas in the Qinling mountains of central China, which seemed, literally, to be the "last refuge" for these charismatic animals. The company continued to embrace new projects worldwide. Two films on lemurs in Madagascar quickly followed and the ring-tailed lemur became the company's logo. Adrian Warren and Dae Sasitorn, who run the company from a farmhouse in Somerset, have created a special website, www.lastrefuge.co.uk, in order to present their work. This is becoming a huge resource for information, and an extensive photographic archive of still and moving images for both education and media. Ultimately they hope to offer special conservation awards to fund work by others.

ADRIAN WARREN

Adrian Warren is a biologist and a commercial pilot, with over 30 years' experience as a photographer and filmmaker. He has worked worldwide for the BBC Natural History Unit, and as a director in the IMAX giant screen format. He has recently designed a new wing-mounted camera system for aircraft to further develop his interest in aviation, aerial filming and photography. As a stills photographer, he has a personal photographic archive of over 100,000 pictures, with worldwide coverage of wildlife, landscapes, aerials, and peoples. His photographs appear in books, magazines, advertisements, posters, calendars, greetings cards and many other products. His awards include a Winston Churchill Fellowship; the Cherry Kearton Medal from the Royal Geographical Society in London; the Genesis award from the Ark Trust for Conservation; an International Prime Time Emmy; and the Golden Eagle Award from New York.

DAE SASITORN

Dae Sasitorn is an academic from the world of chemistry but has given it up to follow her love for the natural world. She manages the company and is a computer expert. She has created, designed and manages the Last Refuge website as well as scanning thousands of images for the archive. She is also a first-class photographer in her own right.

THE PHOTOGRAPHY

Adrian and Dae operate their own Cessna 182G out of a tiny farm strip close to their house. They bought the single engined four-seater aircraft in May 1999 in order to develop a new wing-mounted camera system for cinematography. The 1964 Cessna was in beautiful condition, and had only one previous owner. It is the perfect aircraft for aerial work: small, manoeuvrable, with plenty of power, and the high wing configuration offering an almost unrestricted view on the world below. With 20 degrees of flap it is possible to fly as slowly as 60 knots. The cabin side window opens upwards and outwards and is kept open by the airflow. The photographs were taken on Hasselblad medium format 6 x 6 cm cameras and lenses using Fujichrome Velvia film. Waiting for the right weather, with a clear atmosphere and less than 50 per cent cloud cover, required being on standby for months.

**First Published in 2004 by Myriad Books Limited,
35 Bishopsthorpe Road, London, SE26**

**Photographs and Text ©
Dae Sasitorn and Adrian Warren
Last Refuge Limited**

ISBN 1 904154 87 5

**Designed by Dae Sasitorn and Adrian Warren
Last Refuge Limited
Printed in China**

SOUTH-WEST ENGLAND FROM ABOVE

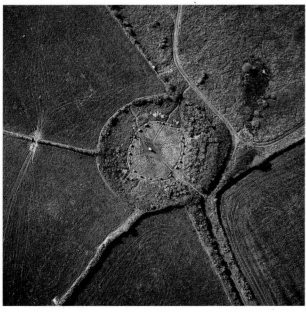

CONTENTS

INTRODUCTION

IN THE SOUTH-WEST OF ENGLAND, the sea is never far away. The region consists of a long peninsula of three counties, Somerset, Devon and Cornwall, each of them steeped in history and legend, of which King Arthur is but one. Here is the southernmost point of England, rolling moorlands, low-lying fen and marshland, spectacular limestone caves and gorges. There are islands, too. The beautiful Scilly Isles off the south-western tip of Cornwall are famed for their mild climate; while Lundy Island, off the northern coast of Devon, is rugged and remote. The climate of the south-west benefits from the warm Atlantic gulf stream, bringing mild, though rather wet weather, all year round. Palm trees and subtropical plants that can survive the winter adorn resorts and private gardens. Holidaymakers flock here to enjoy sandy beaches, rocky coves and quaint fishing villages. Artists and writers come here for inspiration. Local family names can be traced back for centuries. This is indeed a special part of England.

Somerset is bordered on the north by the great estuary of the Severn, and on the south by the English Channel as it widens out to meet the Atlantic. This county is rich in pasture, and Saxon farmers brought their cattle to graze here over 1,300 years ago. If the north coast of Devon is abrupt and dramatic, with high cliffs rising from the Atlantic surf, the south coast is luxuriant and colourful, with a patchwork of fields reaching down to the coast in between the many resort towns and villages. Inland are networks of narrow lanes, winding, climbing and descending steep hills and valleys. Cornwall has an untamed windswept feel to it, with rugged hills, valleys and fields bounded by pale stone walls. Streams rush down to meet the sea in lonely rocky coves, while close by are picturesque fishing villages.

Twelve thousand years ago, Stone Age peoples inhabited caves in the Mendips in Somerset, hunting woolly rhinoceros and other large mammals. Later, Bronze Age peoples constructed timber tracks to cross the Somerset Levels and built stone houses in Cornwall. Stone circles and burial barrows still litter the landscape. The Celts fortified hill after hill in Somerset with massive earthworks to protect their tiny communities from raiders. They were unable to hold out against the Romans however, who left their mark in straight roads, mines, and the famous hot baths of Bath. Castles, abbeys, and lonely church towers are constant reminders of a rich and fascinating past. Everywhere, settlers of long ago have left their traces on the landscape, some of which are best seen from the air.

Photographs from top to bottom: Glastonbury Tor, Restormel Castle, Exeter Cathedral, Boscawen-un Stone Circle

PHOTOGRAPHS, TEXT AND DESIGN BY ADRIAN WARREN AND DAE SASITORN

MYRIAD BOOKS LIMITED

TIN MINES NEAR CAPE CORNWALL (LEFT)

THE GRANITE THAT MAKES UP MUCH OF CORNWALL contains vertical fissures rich in minerals – tin, lead, copper, zinc, iron and silver. The Romans capitalised on it and started a trade that flourished until the 19th century, bringing wealth to coastal villages and ports. The structure of the mineral fissures required a great many deep mines with engine houses to pump out water. Sturdily built, it is these engine houses that survive as ghostly reminders of the past, scattered across the landscape.

TINTAGEL (ABOVE)

LEGEND HAS IT THAT KING ARTHUR was born here in this wild, windswept place on the north coast of Cornwall – A rocky promontory surrounded on three sides by sea and precipitous dark cliffs. There are many ruins here. A Celtic monastery was built around AD500 but abandoned after the Norman conquest. King Arthur's castle was built here in 1145 by the Normans. Originally attached to the mainland, erosion by the sea has worn away the rock so it is reached by climbing steep steps.

ANCIENT PLACES

ANCIENT COMMUNITIES LEFT MANY SIGNS of their
existence on the British landscape. Hill forts, dwellings,
burial chambers, and roads are the most obvious but
dotted here and there are standing stones. Sometimes a
single stone, sometimes a group, sometimes arranged in
rows, sometimes in circles, they have astronomical
significance and offer clues to the beliefs and practices of
peoples who disappeared long ago.

BOSCAWEN-UN STONE CIRCLE (left)
is situated just to the north of St Buryan and
dates back to around 2000BC.

CHYSAUSTER (above) is a remarkably well-preserved
Iron Age village some 3km (2 miles) north of Trevarrack,
believed to have still been in use during the Roman
occupation. It is an example of a courtyard village,
consisting of nine oval stone-built houses, many of them
built in pairs. Each house has a stone-paved courtyard
with a circular living room and smaller rooms off it, which
may have been used for storing food or keeping animals.
The inhabitants made a living by extracting tin from a
nearby river and taking it to merchants at
St Michael's Mount.

CASTLE-AN-DINAS (right) is an Iron Age hill fort with
triple ramparts, only 1km (half a mile) north-west of
Chysauster, which may have had some strategic
connection with the village. Roger's Tower, on the
southern side of the castle, is a folly built around 1800.

CHINA CLAY QUARRIES (ABOVE)

ST AUSTELL IS THE CHINA CLAY CAPITAL of Cornwall. Nearby, great white spoil heaps from the quarries rise like mountains. No wonder they have become known as the Cornish Alps. The china clay, used for the manufacture of countless products from paper to porcelain, and from face cream to paint, as well as some medicines, was discovered here in 1755. It is now one of Britain's major exports and the most important site for its production outside China.

MINACK THEATRE (ABOVE)

"MINACK", IN CORNISH, means "rocky place". Hewn from granite slabs, this wonderful open air theatre is perched on high cliffs overlooking the sea. It is the nearest thing to an ancient Greek theatre, and was the inspiration of Rowena Cade (1893-1983). The first play to be staged here was Shakespeare's *The Tempest* in the summer of 1932. Since then Minack has grown in popularity and now enjoys a worldwide reputation.

LIZARD PENINSULA (LEFT)

THE LIZARD PENINSULA encompasses the southernmost point of England which is not Lizard Point itself but is located much nearer the lighthouse by Polbream Cove. The lighthouse was built in 1753 to keep ships clear of the majestic cliffs and treacherous rocks that extend out from the shore. The name "Lizard" derives from the Cornish word "Lis-Arth" meaning "Holy Palace".

EDEN PROJECT (ABOVE)

THE LARGEST BOTANICAL GARDEN IN THE WORLD opened in March 2001. Dominating the site are the huge biomes: the humid tropics biome, for example, at over 200m long and up to 50m high, is one of the largest greenhouses in the world. It is maintained at a constant 30°C and at high humidity. It contains tens of thousands of plants and trees from the lush rainforests of South America, west Africa, Tropical Islands and Asia. It is a truly ambitious and constantly evolving project.

ST MICHAEL'S MOUNT
(ABOVE AND BACK COVER)

A FEW HUNDRED METRES OFFSHORE FROM
MARAZION in Cornwall, St. Michael's Mount rises
high out of the water. At some time in its history
the island may have been permanently connected to
the mainland, but now it is only possible to walk
across to the island on a causeway at low tide. A
Benedictine monastery was founded here in 1044
by the monks of Mont Saint Michel off the coast of
Brittany to which it bears a close resemblance. Its
potential as a fortress was soon recognised
however, and in 1425 the Crown took control of it.
In 1657, it was bought by the St Aubyn family then,
in 1954, the National Trust acquired it for the nation.

TRURO (RIGHT)

TRURO IS CORNWALL'S ONLY CITY, although
Bodmin is the capital of the county. Truro Cathedral
was completed in 1910, built in the heart of the old
part of the city on the site of the parish church of
St Mary. Many of the materials used, from granite to
copper, were Cornish in origin. In the Middle Ages,
Truro was an important port for the export of
mineral ore. In the 18th century it became a
fashionable place to live and, as a result, has
some fine Georgian houses.

RESTORMEL CASTLE (LEFT)

BUILT IN THE 11TH CENTURY, RESTORMEL CASTLE, near Lostwithiel in Cornwall, is a fine example of a medieval shell keep. By the 13th century it became the property of the Duchy of Cornwall and, as such, belonged to Edward III's son, the Black Prince (1330-1376). In 1644 at the battle of Lostwithiel the castle was captured by Richard Grenville for the King. Sadly, centuries of neglect have taken their toll although a walk through the ruin gives an insight into how it might have looked in its heyday.

PENZANCE (RIGHT)

PENZANCE IS CORNWALL'S OLDEST coastal resort town. Penzance owes its origin to the tin trade and, perhaps, to smuggling. In 1595 the Spaniards burned the town but it was rebuilt quickly only to be ravaged during the Civil War. Penzance was the birthplace of Sir Humphry Davy, the world famous inventor of the miner's safety lamp. Today it is a busy port and starting point for trips to the Scilly Isles.

ST IVES (LEFT)

ST IVES, on the northern side of the Cornish peninsula, is a very picturesque town and is extremely popular with artists. In the 19th century it was a successful pilchard fishing port, and today it is a haven for tourists who come to enjoy the atmosphere of its harbour, its steep narrow streets and alleys, and the surfing beach at Porthmoor.

SCILLY ISLES

THE SCILLY ISLES ARE ONLY 40KM (25 miles) from Land's End but here is a different world, a charming archipelago of 150 islands and islets with clear waters, white sandy beaches and quaint villages. It is a curious fact that more people lived on the islands in ancient times than do now. Of 250 Bronze Age tombs known in England and Wales, 50 are in the Scillies. For centuries smuggling was the main source of income for the peoples of Scilly but now the economy relies largely on the export of flowers and tourism. **TRESCO** (above) is generally considered to be the most beautiful of the islands. The Abbey gardens contain exotic and tropical plants from all over the world.

ST MARY'S (right) is the largest of the islands. The main airport is here as is Hugh Town, with its 18th and 19th century granite buildings.

TAMAR (RIGHT)

TWO BRIDGES SPAN THE TAMAR ESTUARY, linking Plymouth in Devon with Saltash in Cornwall. A marvel in construction, Brunel's famous Royal Albert railway bridge, completed in 1859, now runs in parallel with a road suspension bridge opened in 1961, at the time the longest suspension bridge in Britain. The river Tamar rises close to the north coast and flows southwards for 80km forming the boundary between Devon and Cornwall. The Tamar valley is an area of outstanding beauty.

TORQUAY (BELOW)

DURING THE NAPOLEONIC WARS, the British fleet anchored off Torquay to protect England from invasion. At that time it was just a fishing village, but during the 19th century, with the arrival of the railway, it grew rapidly to become a renowned resort. With its palm trees, stylish houses and moored yachts, Torquay evokes a riviera atmosphere and is one of the most popular west country holiday and retirement destinations.

Dawlish Warren and Exmouth (ABOVE)

ORIGINALLY, DAWLISH WARREN consisted of two parallel sand
spits. A stretch of sand dunes covered by marram grass, it offers
solitude even in summer amid a sea of yellow lupin and views of
Exmouth, in Devon. Exmouth, at the mouth of the river Exe, was a
fishing village that grew into a ferry port in the 13th century. Later,
Sir Walter Raleigh sailed on many of his voyages from here. When
the railway arrived in 1861, it boomed as a holiday resort town.

Castle Drogo (LEFT)

ON THE EDGE OF DARTMOOR, a vast high moorland, Castle
Drogo was designed in 1910 by Sir Edwin Lutyens for Sir Julius
Drewe. It stands on a hilltop site near the village of Drewsteignton
and overlooks the spectacular Devon valley of the river Teign. Sir
Julius had discovered that a Norman baron, Drogo de Teigne, was
his ancestor and was determined to build a castle on the land that
once belonged to him. It was painstakingly constructed from granite
blocks over twenty years and the interior is Medieval in style with
long passageways and a grand staircase.

Exeter cathedral (RIGHT)

ONE OF BRITAIN'S OLDEST CITIES, Exeter is the administrative
capital of Devon. It was founded by the Romans who built a great
red stone wall around it, part of which can still be seen today.
A cathedral was constructed in 1050, and then rebuilt by the
Normans. In the 13th century it was demolished except for the
two towers which were incorporated into the present magnificent
building. Although German bombs flattened most of Exeter in
May 1942, the cathedral miraculously survived.

LUNDY ISLAND (PREVIOUS PAGE)

LUNDY IS SITUATED OFF THE COAST OF NORTH DEVON in the Bristol Channel. A granite outcrop not quite 6km (3.5 miles) long, its western side is braced against the powerful Atlantic swell, with nothing between it and America. With tales of Vikings, pirates and intrigue, the history of Lundy stretches back to Neolithic times. Today there are only a few permanent residents who enjoy island life, which is peaceful and unspoilt. Lundy's flora and fauna is rich and diverse. Most of the island is a Site of Special Interest and many visitors come to watch birds.

SOUTH DEVON COAST

BETWEEN BEER AND BRANSCOMBE is **BEER HEAD** (below), the most westerly white chalk cliff in England. It reaches a height of 130m and has caves that have been used by smugglers. The white chalk has been quarried locally since Roman times, providing the striking white pillars for many Devon churches and for Exeter Cathedral. A few kilometres further west, near Budleigh Salterton, the rock changes dramatically. At **LADRAM BAY** (right), red Permian sandstone crags rise from the sea with evocative names such as the Tower of Babel, the Razor and the Lost World.

LYNTON AND LYNMOUTH
(ABOVE)

LYNMOUTH IS SITUATED where the river Lyn meets the sea; Lynton is perched almost vertically above it, some 165m above the sea. The north Devon scenery here is spectacular with steep ravines, tumbling and cascading river waters and high cliffs. In the Middle Ages Lynmouth was a prosperous herring fishing village although somewhat cut off from the rest of the world. The railway, then roads, started to bring visitors who were attracted by its savage beauty. One night in 1952, after severe rains, the river flooded in a deluge that destroyed Lynmouth, sweeping boulders, trees, houses, cars and people out into the sea.
Many lives were lost.

TAW AND TORRIDGE ESTUARY (LEFT)

THE MOST IMPORTANT DEVON RIVERS flowing into the Bristol Channel, the Taw and the Torridge meet in a common estuary. The river Taw rises on Dartmoor and flows northwards across Devon pastures and finally through the town of Barnstaple. The river Torridge rises far away in Cornwall near the source of the river Tamar, and flows in a wide circuitous route towards Bideford and Appledore where it meets the Taw.

MORTE POINT AND THE NORTH DEVON COAST (ABOVE)

MORTE POINT JUTS OUT INTO THE ATLANTIC from the north Devon coast. Between here and distant Somerset are sheer cliffs up to 300m high. It is a dramatic coastline under constant attack by the powerful Atlantic surf. Small rivers running off Exmoor cut narrow ravines in the cliffs and form plunging waterfalls. There are few villages along this remote, wild and precipitous coast but rocky ledges provide refuges for seabirds.

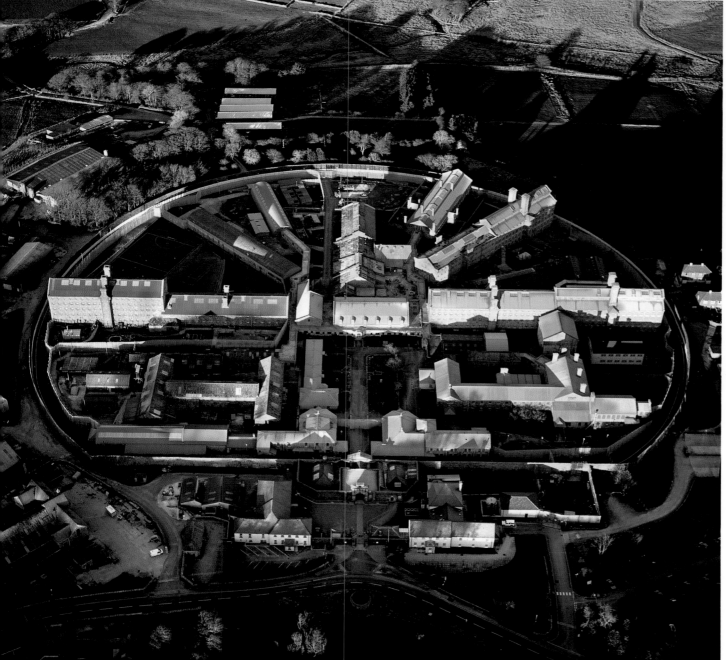

CAPSTONE POINT, ILFRACOMBE
(ABOVE)

ILFRACOMBE IS THE ONLY SEAPORT for large ships on the whole north Devon coast. Its harbour was important throughout the Middle Ages. In the 19th century steamers from here ran regular services to Bristol, South Wales, Ireland and France. The arrival of the railway led to a decline in shipping but tourists began to come, attracted by Ilfracombe's exceptionally beautiful setting, charming natural harbour and elegant Victorian architecture.

DARTMOOR PRISON (LEFT)

THE WORLD FAMOUS PRISON, at Princetown, Devon, was built in 1806 to house French prisoners from the Napoleonic Wars. Between 1812 and 1816 about 1,500 American and French prisoners died in the prison and were buried in a field beyond the prison walls. Some had been brutally mistreated. Unoccupied for over 30 years, Dartmoor was reopened in 1850 as a civilian prison for convicts sentenced to long terms of imprisonment.

DUNKERY BEACON (ABOVE)

THE HIGHEST POINT IN THE NATIONAL PARK of Exmoor rises to 520m. The summit is the site of an ancient warning network, hence the name beacon, where fires were lit to celebrate national events or to warn of possible invasion. Exmoor is renowned for its beauty. Fringed by the north Devon coast with cliffs up to 300m high, Exmoor has wild moorland, ancient forest, valleys, and a rolling patchwork of fields.

DUNSTER CASTLE (RIGHT)

ON THE EDGE OF EXMOOR, Dunster Castle dominates a steep hill overlooking the picturesque village of Dunster. The Castle has only changed hands twice since the Norman conquest of 1066 – the Mohuns until 1376 and the Luttrells from then until 1976 when it was taken over by the National Trust and opened to the public. Nothing now remains of the early buildings but the 13th century gatehouse. The present buildings are of the 17th to 19th century. During the early medieval period the sea reached the base of the hill offering a natural defence, but the sea has slowly receded and it is now several miles away.

BRISTOL (LEFT)

BRISTOL IS THE LARGEST CITY in the south-west of England. It is an important cultural centre with a thriving university community. It grew in Saxon times at the confluence of the rivers Avon and Frome when a bridge was built there and the settlement was called Brigstow. The famous **CLIFTON SUSPENSION BRIDGE** (pictured left) was designed by Isambard Kingdom Brunel, who was also responsible for the Great Western Railway and the SS Great Britain. The suspension bridge, with a span of 214m at a height of 75m above the Avon, was opened in December 1864. Originally intended only for horse-drawn carriages, the bridge now carries 4 million cars each year.

BATH (ABOVE)

NEARLY TWO THOUSAND YEARS AGO, the Romans built their spa of Aquae Sulis around Britain's only hot mineral springs at Bath. The waters are thought to originate from rainwater which fell on the Mendip Hills to the south over 20,000 years ago. They rise from a depth of about 3000m at a constant temperature of 46.5°C. For centuries the healing properties of the hot mineral water have attracted visitors, and led to a unique historic urban environment around the springs. The central area of Bath, now a World Heritage City, is a planned town of Georgian architecture built with liberal use of mellow coloured Bath stone.

GLASTONBURY FESTIVAL
(RIGHT)

IN 1970 MICHAEL EAVIS, of Pilton, decided to stage a music festival on his farm. Today, the Glastonbury Festival is the UK's biggest outdoor pop festival and one of the most famous regular rock festivals in the world attracting well over 100,000 visitors and raising money for charities.

WELLS CATHEDRAL
(BELOW)

WITH A POPULATION OF only about 10,000, Wells in Somerset is the smallest city in England but its cathedral, of which construction began in 1180, is an architectural delight, with a unique scissors arch to support the central tower. The Bishop's Palace, moated home of the Bishop of Bath and Wells, and Vicars Close, a charming 14th-century street joined to the cathedral are among the fine medieval buildings that survive in Wells.

GLASTONBURY TOR (ABOVE)

LEGEND HAS IT THAT JOSEPH OF ARIMATHEA buried the chalice used at the Last Supper at the spring that rises on the slopes of the Tor, a prominent and striking natural hill that rises from the Somerset levels. Excavations have suggested occupation of the hill as far back as the 6th century. A monastery of St Michael existed here early in the medieval period, and terracing on the slopes of the Tor indicates strip lynchets for cultivation from that time. The monastery probably came under the control of Glastonbury Abbey. An earthquake destroyed the church in 1275 but it was rebuilt in the 14th century. At the time of the dissolution of Glastonbury Abbey in 1539, the last abbott and two of his monks were hanged on the Tor. The church became a ruin but the tower was restored in the 18th century. The Tor is in the care of the National Trust.

NETHER STOWEY CASTLE (RIGHT)

AN EARLY NORMAN MOTTE CASTLE was built in the 12th century on the northern fringe of the Quantocks in Somerset by William Fitzodo. It was abandoned in 1485. Not much is left except for the wall foundations of the stone keep which are still visible.

MUCHELNEY (LEFT)

IN A QUAINT VILLAGE on the Somerset Levels are the ruins of a Benedictine monastery, established around AD950. All that exists of the abbey church today are a few foundation walls, but evidence suggests that it was a rather magnificent building. During its history it had been raided by Vikings but survived and indeed flourished until its dissolution in 1532. Then its great abbey church was systematically destroyed and sold for building stone but the abbot's house still stands.

BRENT KNOLL (RIGHT)

AN IRON AGE FORT is located on an isolated hill not far from Burnham-on-Sea. This site was later used by both Romans and the Anglo-Saxons as a refuge against raiding Danes. The interior of the fort has been damaged by quarrying for Lias limestone which caps the hill, and trenches on the northern side were used by military personnel during the Second World War.

SOMERSET LEVELS

THE LEVELS, ONCE INUNDATED BY THE SEA, gradually became a vast area of salt marsh. Prone to **FLOODING** (above), rivers were diverted by settlers, and now a complex network of channels helps drain the land. Frequently swathed in **LOW LYING MIST** (right) that adds a touch of mystery and magic to this place, the Levels are bounded by the uplands of the Mendips, the Quantocks and the Brendon Hills. As long as 6,000 years ago, people built wooden trackways across the marshes to provide access to settlements and hunting areas. At Sedgemoor, in 1685, the last battle to be fought on English soil took place when the Protestant rebellion led by the Duke of Monmouth was defeated by the army of King James II.